Fox's *Adventure*

in Alphabet Town

by *Janet McDonnell*
illustrated by *Jodie McCallum*

created by Wing Park Publishers

CHILDRENS PRESS®
CHICAGO

Library of Congress Cataloging-in-Publication Data

McDonnell, Janet, 1962-
    Fox's adventure in Alphabet Town / by Janet McDonnell ;
illustrated by Jodie McCallum.
      p.   cm. — (Read around Alphabet Town)
    Summary: Fox meets "f" words on his adventure in
Alphabet Town. Includes activities.
   ISBN 0-516-05406-6
   [1. Alphabet—Fiction.   2. Foxes—Fiction.]   I. McCallum, Jodie,
ill. II. Title. III. Series.
PZ7.M478436Fo   1992
[E]—dc 20   91-20546
                                                    CIP
                                                       AC

Fox's *Adventure*

in Alphabet Town

You are now entering Alphabet Town,
With letters from "A" to "Z."
I'm going on an "F" adventure today,
So come along with me.

This is the "F" house of Alphabet
Town. Fox lives here.

Fox likes everything that begins
with the letter "f."

Most of all, Fox likes to go to
the fair.

Every year, Fox meets his friends there. They all bring fine food for a picnic.

Each year, Fox and his friends have fun riding the

Ferris wheel

and playing

football.

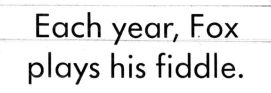

Each year, Fox
plays his fiddle.

One of his friends plays the flute.
Everyone has a fun time!

But one year, four little

fish

had an idea. "Wouldn't it be funny
to make the fountain flood?"

The four fish found a plug. Guess
what happened?

The fountain flooded.

Fox looked down and saw water
flowing everywhere.

He saw everyone and everything
floating away. Away went the
fried chicken and the french fries.

Away went the fudge brownies.
Away went the football.
Away went Fox's friends.

The frogs

did not seem to mind.

And the flamingos just flew
away.

But the others were afraid. "Help!"
they cried. "We are floating away."

"Have no fear," said Fox. And he began to swim for the fountain.

Faster and faster he swam. And with a "foomp," out came the plug.

"Hooray for Fox," everyone said.
"He fixed the fountain."

Just then, the four little fish poked their heads out of the water. "We have been very foolish," they said. "We thought this would be funny.

"We are very sorry."
"Well, you have made a fine mess,"
said Fox. "But one thing is for sure.
This is one fair we will never forget!"

And Fox began to sing,
" 'F' is for a funny fair, with
friends all floating everywhere.

"The fountain flooded. Yes, it's true.
Just look what foolish fish can do."

MORE FUN WITH FOX

What's in a Name?

In my "f" adventure, you read many "f" words. My name begins with an "F." Many of my friends' names begin with "F" too. Here are a few.

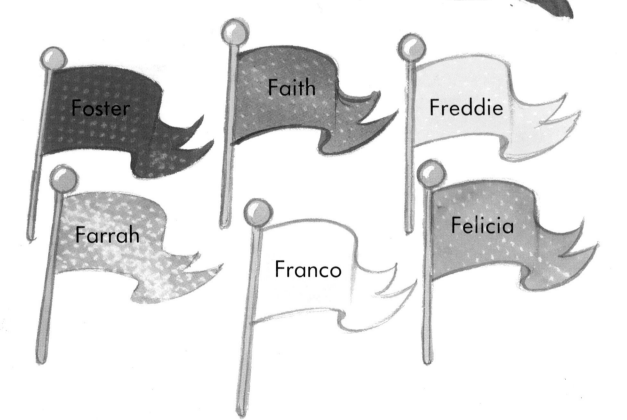

Foster

Faith

Freddie

Farrah

Franco

Felicia

Do you know other names that start with "F"?
Does your name start with "F"?

Fox's Word Hunt

I like to hunt for words with "f" in them. Can you help me find the words on this page that begin with "f"? How many are there?

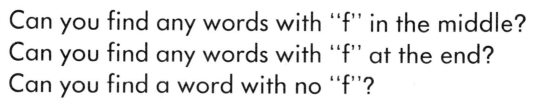

scarf

fire

raft

glove

fork

muffin

flowers

calf

Can you find any words with "f" in the middle?
Can you find any words with "f" at the end?
Can you find a word with no "f"?

Fox's Favorite Things

"F" is my favorite letter. I love "f" things. Can you guess why? You can find some of my favorite "f" things in my house on page 7. How many "f" things can you find there? Can you think of more "f" things?

Now you make up an "f" adventure.